TRAGIC
BITCHES

TRAGIC BITCHES

An Experiment in
Queer Xicana & Xicano Performance Poetry

Adelina Anthony
Dino Foxx
Lorenzo Herrera y Lozano

Kórima Press

"Broken Spanish" appeared in *Mariposas: A Modern Anthology of Queer Latino Poetry* (Floricanto Press, 2008).

"Exotic," "Childhood Dreams" and "Frijol de Temporal" appeared in *Queer Codex: Chile Love* (*allgo*/Evelyn Street Press, 2008).

"Hairspray & Fideo" and "Releasing the X" appeared in *Santo de la Pata Alzada: Poems from the Queer/Xicano/Positive Pen* (Evelyn Street Press, 2005).

"Thirst" appeared in *Toltecayotl Cihuatl* (Mujeres de Maiz, 2006).

Published by Kórima Press
San Francisco, CA
www.korimapress.com

Cover Model: Odyssey Nicole Whitney
Cover Concept: Dino Foxx
Cover Photographer: Troy Wise [www.troywisephotography.com]
Book Design: Lorenzo Herrera y Lozano

Author photograph credits:
Adelina Anthony by Nancy Chargualaf Martin
Dino Foxx by Manuel "Cros" Esquivel
Lorenzo Herrera y Lozano by Orlando Ramírez

ISBN: 978-1-257-10369-0

for our queer ancestras & ancestros
for the generations who follow

CONTENTS

ACKNOWLEDGEMENTS

We are immensely grateful for the support and hard work of all those who were a part of the production of *Tragic Bitches*.

Individuals

Tamara Alvarado
Héctor Bojórquez
Sharon Bridgforth
Manuel Cantú
Tom Capuchin
Micaela Díaz-Sánchez
Melissa Galván
Clifford Gillard
Sarah Guerra
Priscilla A. Hale
Maricella Infante
Karla Legaspy
Allison Moon
Haldun Morgan
Jesús Ortega
Micaela Pérez
Orlando Ramírez
Martha Ramos-Duffer
Marissa Vásquez
Matt Walker
Odyssey Nicole Whitney
Troy Wise
Ofelia Yáñez

Organizations

allgo, a Statewide Queer People of Color Organization
The Historic Victory Grill
Jump-Start Performance Co.
L.A. Gay & Lesbian Center
La Peña Cultural Center
MACLA

Tragic Bitches was performed in the following venues:

La Peña Cultural Center
Berkeley, CA
May 6, 2007

Movimiento de Arte y Cultura Latino Americana (MACLA)
San José, CA
November 8 & 9, 2007

L.A. Gay & Lesbian Center
Hollywood, CA
November 10, 2007

allgo, a Statewide Queer People of Color Organization
The Historic Victory Grill
East Austin, TX
March 23, 2008

INTRODUCTION:

A tragedy is born...

It all began on a second-hand couch, by the light of aging candles and to the sound of old boleros. The artists, feeding off sundried cranberries and sipping corner-store wine, reminisced, lamented and laughed at the agony of memory. Void of innocence and replete with desolation, *Tragic Bitches* was born.

Tragic Bitches was an experiment, an attempt to dance with the demons of our past and the solace of our present. As poets of broken and fractured homes, our pens are calloused, our bodies the anamnesis of loss. We unveiled the ink-drenched cloth of shame to reveal the tragic moments that stain as much as manteca dripping from midnight tacos in bed.

Resisting legacies of familial silence and community censorship, we sought to dive into the darkest, most corrupt of our poet selves. We sought to scrape the elbows of memory by embracing the sorrow of mutilated loves, dilapidated childhoods and corroded dreams. Collectively, we began to weave together the somber worlds from which we write.

Once on stage, we seduced and coerced others to sit in the mud of our tragedies. We created the illusion of backyard tardeadas, of plastic-covered couches and of hidden cantinas. We nestled our poetic serenades in the rhythms of aching rancheras, demanding hip hop beats and indelible oldies. As churches of archaic and colonizing rituals, we gave name to a poet's place of worship.

Far too chaotic to be spoken word, *Tragic Bitches* was conceived as performance poetry. We were poets in performance, performers of a rhymeless script. We envisioned a world trapped between revered juke joints and despised hipster coffee shops. We betrayed the writer within us, exposed the reclusive process and fed the voyeurs before us.

Tragic Bitches was an experiment. Unscientific and flawed, we are uncertain of our success. Still, we dared open the doors of prevailing closets and threw our defiled laundry to the wind. We made love to the past, retaliated against the moment.

This book is the continuation of our experiment. In it, you will find the poems stumbled upon, performed and whispered into the ears of others. You will find the songs woven within movement and poetry. You will find our stories.

As the prying audiences touching the nudity of our vulnerability, we welcome you to caress the scars left on these pages. We recognize that our story is the story of many. Perhaps our story is your story.

Come, traipse the dark corners of these poetic memories.

Dile al que te pregunte que no te quise;
dile que te engañaba, que fui lo peor.

José Ángel Espinoza "Ferrusquilla"
Échame a Mí la Culpa

CANELA SWEET ERUPTIONS

YOU BRING OUT THE JOTO IN ME

you bring out the Joto in me
the María Felix eyebrows
the sexually confused macho
the Tecate & lime
the Saturday morning shock
of hickies and phone numbers
you are the one I would hold hands
in public with, while cruising down my old barrio
allow you other men in bed, still believing
promises of monogamy and forever
definitely
definitely
for us

you bring out the Chelo Silva in me
the bolero in me
la mano caída, tight jeans and spiked hair in me
the velvet dress on a Sunday morning,
unshaved legs with white nylons in me
the spine of Frida in me
the butchered Coyoxauqui in me
the screaming super market baby in me
the government cheese in me
the chismoso y metiche in me
the fetish of crucifixes on a hairy chest in me
the J pronounced as Y in me
the greasy, mullet-like wavy hair in me
the Chihuahua desert, pecans and red meat in me
the love of death in me
you know you do
oh, you know you do

you bring out the drag queen in me
the perpetual attitude in me
the Juan Gabriel trip and fall in me
the Rivera-inspired Catrina in me
the gay bar bathroom bump in me

the *Bidi-Bidi-Bom-Bom* in me
the San Antonio 3:00 a.m. fideo con carne in me
the fondling on the dance floor in me

papacito, my sweet obsession
I am the psycho who stalks your home at night,
make sure you're there when you say so
I would find a man just to cheat on him with you
I want to bottom, top, flip it and reverse it, with you
I want to commit unforgivable sins and bask in them
I want to trade Grey Goose for Boones Farm,
coke for crack, Banana Republic for the Gap
me sacas lo maricón en mí, y te gusta, chulo

you bring out the ojo-giving celoso in me
the "I'm gonna cut her if he don't stop starin' at you" in me
the high-heel-stabbing Esta Noche draga in me

the blank-stares at football games in me
the Texas syphilis breakout in me
the AIDS pandemic in me
the Out Magazine never seen Mexican cover-boy in me
I'd mispronounce my name for you
light a cigarette and watch how others lust for you,
ready to burn whoever gets too close

sabes que soy cabrón
soy San Lorenzo quien quema los pies de noche
I am the excessive drinker
the insatiable size-queen
the sex-addicted promiscuity
you bring out the superficial lust-at-first-sight in me
the vile jealousy in me
the voyeur and exhibitionist in me
the leather daddy in me

sage, Pomada de la Campana, Concha Nacar
hierbaloca, Jabón ZOTE, mota, Sal de Uvas
lavender candles
all you locas, talented and not,
Marisela Monet, Kelly Kline, represent girls

I want to be your loca
only your papi
be my papi
I want to show you the way jotos do it
the way we were meant to

LOVING HOMEGRRRL

Loving my homegrrrl
might mean when I say,
Damn, estás chula, mamita!
that she goes,
Whatever…

No, for realz, just beautiful!
& she goes,
Shut-up…

Bueno, pues, estás fea…
& that's when homegrrrl
finally says,
Ah, baby, I love you!

Loving homegrrrl in this new way:
a mix of street attitude in the lingo
with canela sweet eruptions of cariño,
might mean our closest comadres say,
(à la María Félix raised eyebrow y todo)
What?! Are they scamming now?

It's all good this mad luv & concern
cuz "party grrrl" & "post-heartbroken"
seem like a recipe for destruction.
Too many friendships martyred —
in our circle of old lovers now friends
old friends with another's old ex
& new lovers turned quickly into haterz.
It's that tired old fate of embittered queridas
playing the role again of *ay, la sufrida.*
The she don't talk to her — or her or her!
Our circles broken & mended & broken.
It's the YMCA dance of the wayward
homo-chromosomes.

So, de veras, it's all good,
your mad luv & concern.
Cuz we have it too.

We know wounds fester
& yeah, up to now…
we've only been homegrrrls.
But, damn, she brought the poetry back
when the metaphors were deep-buried
under pliable rain-soaked tejas tierra
cuando yo ya no creía o quería
she resuscitated the Spanglish lyricism
& my belief that one well-placed vowel
birthed from our cultura of elongation
as in *"Whaaaaaaat?"*
can hold all of life's surprising mysticism;
like those mariposa besos of hers, soft as drizzle
that slowly moistened this once brittle corazón.

Homegrrrl, loving you is not always easy.
We've got throbbing & living histories.
We too have acted suspiciously,
cuz you've seen my game &
I've heard about yours.
Coqueta, should be your Christian name.

But still — between us — there's confianza.
We share moments too delicious
for homegrrrls to accept as nada.
Es mucho más…

That makes us fragile
a preemie love?
Cuz we didn't want it
born
not yet
maybe later
much much later.
But here it is
fighting for each breath
& surviving

cuz loca homegrrrls
don't quit on each other.
I got your back.
You got mine.
You got me, mujer,
just in time…
you
  get
    me.

I'm loving you
homegrrrl
& loving me
so don't worry
just continue to be
firework at the fiesta
a buttery nipple drink
& a muy MySpace diva.
Let the mundo think
anything & everything,
cuz I got your back
& I'm placing my lips,
my breasts & soft belly
against it… feel it?

8

EXOTIC

I fell in love with a boy.
I fell in love once and I lost completely.

See, he was in love with a girl.
I fell in love with a straight boy.
A heterosexual, better called "heteroflexible."
The only difference between this guy and a gay guy
Is a six-pack of Shiner Bock.

The view from inside the closet must be getting old.
I'm surprised the walls haven't started to
Close in on you yet.
Kindly be a dear and hand me my coat,
It's time for me to go out.
I keep wishing you would follow my lead
And leave that dark,
Damp place to see the light of the world and what it could be
For you and me…but it won't happen and I can't make it happen.
I don't wanna be your exotic, homoerotic,
Man-whore, boy toy fantasy.

I can't be seduced by your half-bred,
Frat boy, truck driving, faded t-shirt wearing,
Low rise Levi jeans sportin', straight porn watching charm.

Don't let yourself be seduced by my difference.
Don't build your fucked-up fetish fantasy around
The sway of my hips as I walk away from you.
My milkshake does bring all the boys to the yard, but come on.
I don't wanna be your exotic, homoerotic,
Man-whore, boy toy fantasy.

I can no longer sit around waiting for you to feel on again,
Won't sit here with my thumb up my ass while you feel off again.
Don't expect me to come running to the phone
When you decide to call and don't expect me to
Shove my tongue down your throat
When you've finally had enough to drink.

I don't wanna be your exotic, homoerotic,
Man-whore, boy toy fantasy.
I'm sick of your Almond Joy,
"Sometimes ya feel like a nut,
Sometimes ya don't" bullshit mentality.
There are lots of tricks out there that
Would be more than willing to let you use them.
Why did you choose me?

The rhythm with which I move as I stroll
Ain't some spicy, delicious, Latin beat,
It's just a walk, get over it.

I don't wanna be your exotic,
Homoerotic, man-whore, boy toy fantasy.
Don't wanna be your Mr. Slave, slut bag,
Skank weed, chew toy, circle jerk, j/o buddy,
Reach around machine, cum hole, fuck hole,
Little piece of the Latin Invasion.
Cuz odds are, if I made you step outside
Your little hiding spot, I would have to raise you
Like some sort of gay mother.
Teaching you the things you learn when you
Finally come out and stop pretending.
It would be as if you were born again and
I don't have time to teach someone how
To live their life when I don't exactly know
How to live my own.

I don't wanna be your first.
Don't wanna be your breathe of fresh air,
Your taste of the new world.
I deserve someone who doesn't
Turn me on and off like a light switch.
Don't want to be your exotic.

FRIJOL DE TEMPORAL

bendita sea la sensación
que me brota como el frijol
sembrado en mala temporada
apenas lo rosa el sereno
y pa' pronto se para
esa sensación cuando un moreno
me coquetea de pasada

una mirada no más
basta pa' quedarme maduro
como membrillo listo pa' cajeta
como chile ancho pa' rellenos
como elote pa' chacales
como arado pa'l surco

bendita sea la sensación
si me suele alborotar
como culebra de potrero
como perro enrabiado
como buitre en pleno invierno
embriagado como gusanito
en agua ardiente en tiempos de progreso

si me llega a tocar
que se aliste pa'l susto
la Llorona no se me compara
cuando ando en busca de un buen gusto
me sale lo Juana Gallo
igual de fiera e igual de brusco

si me chifla a ese son
ese que incita bajo el calzón
lo picoteo como un huisache
hasta que quede como cedazo
enredado sobre mi estandarte
que pa' evitar mis espinas
no existe guarache

BLESSED AND STAIN-WORTHY

SANTA PANOCHA

These days deseo las católicas
believers of prayer & milagros.
Womyn who always whisper
Hail Marys & Our Fathers
with labios pressed urgently
against the soft pyramid
of my brown mestiza pelos.
Deep inside my dark, copal scented templo
fire-tongues flick in fury
like the wick of a belly-dancing flame.
& the womyn scream too
much like you did during worship
Omigod, omigod, omigod!
Righteously,
conflating my name
with divinity.
Yes, I confess
my sins of lust,
revenge & hubris.

abrazarte quisiera, aunque había noches
cuando no quería tu boca sobre mi pecho
ahora quiero olvidarte en otra religión
porque tú no tuviste fe ni compasión

When the followers come on their knees
hungry for salvation, I dutifully part my lips.
In this act of self-redemption... *Here's my body.*
They greedily swallow a small wafer already
melted down to a milky pearl & follow this
with sanguine kisses, blessed & stain-worthy,
because the sheets we used to make love on
have been burnt by a new lover's urgency.

abrazarte quisiera, aunque había noches
cuando no quería tu boca sobre mi pecho
ahora quiero olvidarte en otra religión
porque tú no tuviste fe ni compasión

With ardent thumbs & forefingers,
like a rosary, womyn rub my nipples.
Instantly — I become church choir
Alleluia! Praise be the Mujeres!
Between my legs
they deliver ecstasy on a higher octave; sabes…
We bite, grind, & rebuke your image
& only once, did I forsake one of them
by imagining you & the heavens
we once shook & made rumble.

abrazarte quisiera, aunque había noches
cuando no quería tu boca sobre mi pecho
ahora quiero olvidarte en otra religión
porque tú no tuviste fe ni compasión

I gently lift my Catholic girls reeking of sex
kiss their scabbed knees & then taste myself
on fideo thin lips & there I begin to find
forgiveness.
For you. Me. All of us.
I wish you well on your pilgrimage
as you seek other delicate gods & goddesses.
The death pangs I suffered for you have been worn-down
like the wood of tired pews that hold up sinners.
Keep your soul.
Keep your tears.
& pseudo loyalty.
I have found that there are plenty who believe
In holiest of all my mythologies,
mi Santa Panocha, cabrona… querida

BROKEN SPANISH

I will fuck you in broken Spanish
I will not conjugate verbs correctly
And try to cover it up by performing
Those actions over and over in
Different positions

I will get nervous and sweat, and trip and,
Mispronounce words on your skin
As I travel from your neck down to
Your smooth chest down to your furry
Tummy down to the soles of your feet

I will confuse my tenses and will
Fuck you with no concept of past,
Present or future, taking out aggression
From past lovers — forget who I was
Fucking, and set concrete plans for
Our next encounter

I will overcompensate for my poor
Pronunciation and roll my tongue
With full force as I eat your ass
Leaving my goatee smelling of
Your sweetness for me to enjoy on
The drive home

I will mix up masculine words with
Feminine words. Confuse you the top
With me, the versatile bottom. Flip you
Over and make love to your furry
Ass with no apologies

I will speak to you in every Spanish
Accent I've ever heard. Go from
"Órale chulo, bésame bien fuerte" to
"O sea, ay güey, ¡no mames!" to
"Coño, carajo, come on papi, lemme
See dat cum." "¡Sas culera!"

I will fuck you in broken Spanish
In the only way I know how;
And you will enjoy it, like a hot
Pot of fideo from Mama's kitchen —
To be eaten with hot, homemade
Cornbread and sliced jalapeño

CHILDHOOD DREAMS

when I grow up
I don't wanna be Hispanic
'cuz my land may be occupied
my body may be invaded
and I may only speak European languages
but I decide what I call myself

and when anybody tries to make me check that box
I'm checking "other"
and I'll do it with red eyeliner too
just in case
anybody has any doubts
of how I am not
Hispanic

when I grow up
I wanna be a good Mexican American
even better than Linda Ronstadt
'cuz I don't only sing in Spanish
I speak it too

I wanna be so good at being a Mexican American
that when I get kicked out of a hotel
for dedicating one of my poems to Michael Moore
they will know
that an invitation to come back
and sing the national anthem with him
is not an apology
'cuz I don't sing the war song of the occupier
but I will graffiti my ass on their lobby walls
just in case
anybody has any doubts
of just how good
a Mexican American I am

when I grow up
I wanna be queer
I wanna be so damn queer
that even the queer think I'm queer

yeah
that's how queer I wanna be
I wanna dye my hair crazy colors
shake my ass excessively as I walk
speak with a hint of a lisp
just in case
anybody has any doubts
of just how
queer I am

when I grow up
I wanna be a fierce Xicano
with an x
don't ask why
it just sounds better
¿y qué?

I wanna be so damn Xicano
that every time I fuck a man
he'll find Aztlán all over me
just in case
anybody has any doubts
of how fierce
a Xicano I am

cuando yo sea grande
quiero ser mexicano
I wanna be so Mexican
que mi abuela won't be able to blame the US
for her grandson being a fag
porque yo aprendí a mamar verga en tierra mexicana

I wanna show the scars under my fingernails
the mesquite scratches on my face
and the tears of my soul
let those be my passport back home
just in case

LORENZO HERRERA Y LOZANO

anybody has any doubts
of just how
Mexican I am

cuando yo sea grande
I wanna make my daddy proud
I wanna go to a university
that isn't even capable of pronouncing our name right
I wanna wreak havoc
pronounce my last name with a silent "h"
and roll my "r's" so hard
they'll wanna call la migra on me
just in case
anybody has any doubts
of how proud
my daddy is of me

when I grow up
I wanna be an activist
I wanna fight with my gente
I wanna join arms with my sisters and brothers
I wanna tie myself naked to the doors of the Texas Capitol
so tight
Governer Perry won't know if he should blow me
or oppose the death penalty

I wanna fight for liberation
for true liberation
I wanna be so busy fighting for the right to live
that I wont have time to fight for the right to marry
to buy another house
or take another cruise
I wanna fight against the real issues
the core of our oppressions
just in case
anybody has any doubts
of what kind of
activist I am

---

cuando yo sea grande
quiero ser poeta
I wanna write some fucking poems
that is
poems about fucking
not about making love

I'm talking some raunchy
hombre a hombre
"get on your knees
papi chulo
worship & suck"
kinda poems

I wanna write so many fucking poems
that the day the church
gets a hold of 'em
they're gonna run outta ways to masturbate
just in case
anybody has any doubt
of what kind of
poet I am

HIGHKICKS & HANDCUFFS

You can keep your overpriced fancy
Aloha register and your broken tip jars
But we're keeping the memories of
Endless nights we spent dancing to the
Beat pouring through the speakers
Under a blanket of flashing lights and
Spinning mirrors.

You can keep your bartenders that
Are way too cute to be mad at for not
Knowing how to pour a strong drink
But we'll keep the money we would
Have spent on bottomless Absolute
Citron Cape Cods and trust bitch,
That's a lot of money.

You can keep my VIP Gold Card
But we'll keep the memory of being
Complete rock star divas and of skipping
Ahead of the line that wrapped around
The block and the looks on all of the
Bitter constipated queens' faces, who had
Been in line for 30 minutes as we
Were rushed on by them to be let
In without paying cover.

You can keep your Video Bar that
Played all of our guilty pleasures
But you can't take away the rhythm
In our hips that seduced countless
Men on that silver dance floor nor
Can you take away the night that
I ended up on my back staring at
The ceiling after trying to dance
Like a Britney Spears back-up
Dancer in chanclas.

You can keep your main dance
Floor with all of your shirtless
White boys jumping around
To rhythmless music but we'll
Keep the times we laughed at
The entire room for jumping up
And down at the same time during
The chorus of Kelly Clarkson's
Since You've Been Gone and
The *más* hot attitude we would
Throw while learning to hold
Complete conversation while
Not breathing and keeping our
Stomachs sucked in. *Purple*
Is our color anyway, gurl.

You can keep your grand ballroom
On the third floor and your bad
Lighting but we'll keep the fun we
Had in the hidden restroom and
The funky fresh way we impressed
The whole party with the way we
Leaned with it, and rocked with it
And popped & locked from left
To right and snapped our fingers
And how we leaned back. Word.

You can keep your photo booth
That is mostly used for minors to
Sneak drinks to enhance their
BX experience but we'll keep
The countless photos we have of
Us in drag on Halloween or of us
Doing dirty things with our
Rosaries and we'll take with us
The memories we have of the
Many boys we kissed in random
Places around the club.

You can keep your flying chanclas
And angry ex boyfriends trying to fight
But we'll keep the countless after-hours
In horrible lighting at house parties or
Las Salsas or Mi Tierra or Mr. Taco
With menudo, or fideo con carne, Big Red,
Drag queens and carne guisada con cheese.

When SAPD squad car 7334 drove away
With my heart and my life in the backseat
You tried to rob us of 8 years of history.
We find ourselves trying to shake
You like a bad dream but these memories
Remain there like stretch marks, sad
Little reminders of decadent nights of
The past.

We're forced back down on the strip
Going to bars that smell like arroz con culo
Or bars that only play good music when
They are trying to make a quick buck
Off our people by bringing in a random
Pop en Español artist. There's a huge
Hole in our hearts because of this but
We'll wait until the memories of the
High kick seen around the world fade
Or we're too famous for you to care
And we'll once again return to church
For the kind of prayers that can only
Be heard above the loud music of
The Bonham Xchange.

BITTER AND SWEET

YOU NEVER CHANGE

You taste bitter and sweet.
You taste that way because you are poisonous.
Poison will kill you
Or at least make you throw up.
That is what this poem is.
It is my purging of thoughts and of your negative energy.
But poison will do something wicked.
It does make you vomit like after hours of crying hysterically
When you broke my heart for what I swore was the last time
Or after drinking too much alcohol straight from the bottle
Trying my best to believe that you no longer exist.
Bringing you back into my life would be like poisoning
My tired nights with belligerent
"I've always loved you," text messages
And "Can I come over?" drunk dials.

I can't take you back because weak people
Don't change like they do in the movies, and
My head hurts from constantly beating it against a wall.
Closing my eyes as you kiss my erogenous zones won't
Blind me from the reality that you will always go back to
her when you are sober and hung over in the morning.
I am lonely at night with no one in my bed,
But asking you to come over to cuddle would
Bring me back to falsely loving you with a body
That needs to find meaning again.
I could call every time I'm reminded of an inside joke
We shared but that would put me back in a rut where
Things repeat themselves and we repeat ourselves
And fight more than we kiss.

Facing your demons is important. But, what's the point
Of facing your demons if you turn around and sleep
With them every night?
Why would I continue to hurt myself over you?
You won't ever love me.
You will only use me for sexual gratification

That will lead to further complication
When your girlfriend catches me in bad mood
And I corner her to explain how you
Suck dick better than any man I've ever met.

     Yeah, I know, two wrongs don't make a right,
     But sometimes slashing his tires makes you feel better.

I can let you sweet talk your way back in with
Thoughts of how things should have been, but slowly
The phone calls stop and I have to relive the way it
Really was, no matter how much it hurt. And you will
Be nowhere to be found even though you promised
Not to leave again.

I could surrender and let you seduce me into your
Bedroom once more but I know that he is going
To eventually come back to town from vacation wanting his
Boyfriend back and even you though you told me
He was only your friend you'll somehow miraculously
Lose my phone number and I won't hear from you again
Until you're ready to get a lovin' you obviously ain't
Getting from him.

I promise you, I'm not as dumb as you think I am.
What you failed to realize is that I am a vessel of
Light and creation that is sent to spread the
Word of a revolution that doesn't include scared-ass,
Motherfuckin' punk ass bitches like you, who love
To make excuses for simply not knowing what they want
From the world, and who take up too much
God damned space,
Adding nothing new or positive to the world and stealing
Oxygen from the rest of us who could really use it.
One of these days you'll wake up and learn that you
Missed out on something good. You'll find yourself
remembering the sweet words I spoke,

the way my jaw pops out of
Place and that I don't have a gag reflex
And I'll simply slip you a bit of your own poison
And laugh as you scream in pain.
You won't get any help from me, and you will
Wonder why I don't call back.
You ain't the only one who can lose a
Phone number, bitch.

MEDIA GOTA DE TEQUILA

te dejo el desmadre que tú mismo
fuiste a escarbar con devoción
para que aproveches el resultado de tu egoísmo
para que sientas la falta que hago yo

te dejo media gota de tequila
el resto lo bebí con tu honor
al fin que ni falta le ha de hacer a tu méndiga vida
lo mismo que no te hizo falta mi cariño
media gota te ha de bastar como lo hice yo

de tus noches me llevo las estrellas
que te ilumine el desconsuelo
duerme sólo con la pena
que te cubra el frío como un día yo

la hora que comiences a añorarme
búscame en el fondo del horror
el infierno en que tú me arrojaste
que venga a rescatarte tu cinismo
que ni para enterrarte regreso yo

BROKEASS LOVE

Racing, rushing, zooming
Racing, rushing, zooming
Swift goodbyes & besos
Another skipped breakfast
Grrrl, who's got time to cook
Tortillas con chorizo y huevo?
You gotta go & I gotta go,
All these deadlines are looming
Really, who's got room for us?

We pencil in our "quality" time
make do with a few minutes
on hurried weekday nights
& miraculously, sometimes,
we get to chillax on the weekend,
maybe some quick, unexpected sex;
that's if we haven't already pissed
each other off cuz pms-ing & the stress
over familia & the bills, the bills, the bills,
& the fact we no longer feel connected.

Hmmm...
we wonder how we lost that special loving
like walking through that Guerneville forest
where the Kodak pictures we took said
this non-state sanctified marriage is legit
te acuerdas? it all started with swapping spit
& story on an iron-wrought bed
we made ritual out of talk & touch
& with the snore of tren
temblando through darkness
we fell nightly into deep
purple room sueños

But now it seems impossible to relish
this new house, this summer stillness
this quiet doesn't connote peace

hearts mute & numb & fo' sure,
not feeling closer than before;
I am forgetting the scent of lavender on your neck
you are forgetting to kiss the harps on my wrists
we forgot those silent messages we wrote
on the palms of our hands, letter by letter.

& we SWORE
we'd never be that
but here we are
another casualty
a loveless couple
cuz every precious minute
too valuable to spend it
we cannot deal with our mess
forget the long-term investment
we're content with the unpredictability
of the market: up today, down yesterday

& baby, I'm telling you
when life comes to take away
what we tried to create
something singular, unique
between two overworked mujeres,
we'll watch with red-red eyes as
as it's carried off piece by piece
we'll stand there... ay, qué pendejas
heartbroken & yeah, broke-ass.
with more than enough
time
to wonder
were all of your meetings
worth-while?
& my days with these words...
Ever. Well. Spent?

HUMAN, SPIRITUAL AND FLAWED

HAIRSPRAY & FIDEO

growing up
the only smell I held dearer
than 'Macita's burnt fideo
was the smell of Aqua-Net

the kind of smell that lingered
long enough to cause a fire
when one of my college-bound uncles lit a fatty

those were the days
when 'Macita would warn me of the cholo neighbors
that dressed and acted like my tíos

and when I'd mention this similarity
she'd say
tus tíos no son cholos
they just dress that way

back then 'Macita would spend hours
talking to tía Nona from Monterrey
about so-and-so's daughter
who got pregnant before marrying
and about a cousin of a cousin of a cousin
of the neighbor who had a dog
who bit the old man that owned the corner store
when they were growing up
was moving to San José
so we should expect a call
he must of called collect cuz 'macita never accepted

yeah, those were the days
when Ken would grind the camouflage off G.I. Joe's ass
while my cousins weren't looking
when they were looking
I'd comb Barbie's hair
drown her in a cloud of Aqua-Net
and take off in her corvette

cuz we didn't need no man
telling us what to do

that was before lip-syncing to
La Isla Bonita became uncool
before Barbie lost her hair due to all the hairspray
and Ken and G.I. Joe went their separate ways
to a segunda

that was before we had to grow up
forget by means of ridiculing the past
of not being caught dead speaking Spanish
outside 'Macita's house

our brown growing pains
didn't happen overnight
they happened all the time
they happened when we learned that tíos
going to college meant they were going to prison
and that's why 'Macita wouldn't accept collect calls
when we realized nobody in our family
had ever been to a university and that maybe
it wasn't going to be that easy for us to go

maybe the tíos in college had a point
things aren't that easy for us
maybe the reason Ms. Nelson treated me like shit
in her second grade class was because
I didn't belong there
or did I?

oh, but the years have passed
some primas got pregnant before marriage
some never married – the lucky ones
some primos are still in the closet
tíos finally came home from college

LORENZO HERRERA Y LOZANO

and I became a full-blown queen — convinced
that camouflage is no longer sexy
and that Herbal Essence hairspray
does not have the same healing powers as Aqua-Net

| THE FAMILY

At the base of the loma that stretches up
To Memorial High School sits a two-story
Blue and white house. Grandma has been
Gone for years now and the house sits
Filled with memories, occupied by
Tía Nancy. La Nasarita, never married
Because she always has to have things her
Way and no man was going to ever
Change that. Human, spiritual and flawed
Wrapped up in feminine clothing and sealed in
A thin layer of Rave hairspray. The only
Tía who would give the nieces and nephews
All the love in her heart because she had
No children of her own. She marches to the
Beat of her own drummer and always knows
How to talk me down when mom and I fight.
I want to be just like her when I grow up.

Tradition runs deep in my family. My house
Is filled with furniture passed down from
Generation to generation, from one house
To the next (and you best not give this shit
Away to someone outside of the family
Or to someone the family has since stopped
Talking to over some random fight or the other
Because you'll get some rowdy looks from
The Tías that sit around grandma's mesa in the
Kitchen, eating too much and gossiping
Like good Southern Christian women do).
It all stays in the family, like silence, like
Bad habits, like diabetes, like cancer, like
Ignorance, like homophobia, like forced
Christianity, like attitude, like bad tempers,
Like ignoring the bad with fake happiness,
Like alcoholism, like pill popping, like self-
Diagnosis, like thinking that all men can be

Good men after a little molding and he'll
Stop cheating on you or hitting you if you
Pray hard enough.

Grandpa cheated on Grandma the way
My dad cheated on my mom, and the way
All men have cheated on me. I'll gladly
Accept the solid oak coffee table that was
Passed down to me de la casa de 'uelita.
I'll even take the old upright piano that
I used to annoy my mom with growing up
When I have a house big enough to fit it in.
I want my madrina's collection of music
Boxes, quiero la cama de la casa de mi padrino,
Y también quiero la mesa de mi Tía Nancy,
Para poder continuar la tradiccion de puro
Pinche chisme. But I'll break the cycle of abuse.
At least I'll try.

I'll remember the man that touched Madrina
Inappropriately. I'll remember that she was
Was locked away and strapped to a bed. I'll
Remember how father pinned mom to the bed.
I'll remember how he'd whip her face with his
Belt. I'll remember Joe. I'll remember what
He looked like when he was angry. I'll
Remember the way his voice sounded when
He yelled. I'll feel his weight pressed
Against my body as he tried to get inside.
I'll remember the way his face looked
Through the tears. I'll never forget these things
The next time I find myself trying to be more
Like one of my dumb primas as opposed to being
Like la Tía Nancy, who needed no man to
Change her.

THIRST

Not yet sprawling: San Antonio
You had dreams of moving there
of leaving that Pleasanton rancho
where your daughter days were stolen
by the man you called apá

Too young, too female to be heard
once, you tried running away
rapid deer legs of a twelve-year old
with a mist of fog for camisole
hunted, captured, returned by your hermano
You, niña, would not shame them with your escape
insisting on something more for yourself

Back to the broken house where floorboards
creaked with those shuffling footsteps
of living death,
of nightmares,
of calloused hands…
dick
penetrating baby flesh
abandoned by all to wallow wounded
asustada in your burgeoning womanhood

Many, many years later, he, like others,
who came from Durango, Jalisco,
Oaxaca, Michoacán,
from who knows where…
he saw you
behind the jealous shadow of your father
& he wondered what your mouth tasted of

Because hunger recognizes itself
you found ways to escape Father-Brother-Primo
vigilant ojos always watching
your promiscuous puta ways

but hunger devours & never asks
you made yourself naked to this Mexican
Man of promises & lovemaking by theft

Famished, you took him
your legs held his waist, hard
something like an abrazo between womyn friends
all night you cradled his immigrant dreams
in your third generation Tejana sex
you confused his Mexican tongue
& trabajador sweat
for something
to call yours

What did he promise you?

I know he lied

That's what they told me
part of the untold truth
que he married you for a green-card
for a way to feed his familia
his other wife & huercos
allá en México…

It's what his compadres confirmed
when you went to that single apartment
on South Flores Street, & entered
a coffin of a room
where ten migrant workers slept
minus the one you searched for

I don't know when
or if you ever told him
about me

Were you ashamed of me?

That I too was inside of you
my hands, my skin, my heart,
for nearly a year
only you
seed of my woman-to-woman desire

Eventually,
you chose me,
over him,
over betrayal,
over your family

You chose not to drink a tea
that would have cramped your insides
would have held the idea of me
in an unforgiving fist for hours
& then would have released
me as crimson flower
blood & tissue dripping
between your legs

I see now
this want of me
was somehow
your most lesbian act ever

I never had a choice
but to love you &
that warm woman bruised
cuerpo of yours
I tasted generations
of putrid historia
each time your breasts
nourished me with your
llanto-stained milk

       ADELINA ANTHONY

y mamá… your hurts still live in me

I, the lesbian daughter,
who drank of you
do not forget

SED POR UN CONSUELO

HOLLOW

I am only the shell of the man
That my parents wish I were
So it's a complete surprise
That I bleed as much as I do
When you cut me.

I am hollow, so when you
Place me to your ear you can
Actually hear the sounds of
My broken past.

Sounds of breaking glass, holes
Being kicked into walls, and
Deep voices shouting into the
Night are amplified by father's
Rage.

If you listen carefully, you can
Hear the softest of sounds, like the
Needle slowly stitching up Mama's
Forehead right at her color treated
Hairline where Father broke open
A 40oz beer bottle.

You can place your ear to my
Chest and hear Mama's soft voice
As she teaches us the made-up
Story to explain to guests how
The holes got into the wall.

You can hear seagulls and the waves
Of the Gulf of Mexico crashing onto
The Texas coast just down the sandy
Hill from our condo, where we would
Play perfect family.

You can hear the sound of a bowl
Crashing into the sink, and Mama's
Voice screaming about how she
Sacrificed everything, and risked
Her life too many times to have
Her son not get into heaven for
Being gay.

You can hear Tía's voices ask if
I ever plan on finding a woman
To marry and in the same breath
Ask if I have any suggestions
For window treatments to match
The new couch.

You can hear the sound of a fist
Hitting bare skin and the loud voice
Of the first man who ever hit me
Right before he tried to rob me of
An innocence that had been long
Gone.

You can hear my tears falling into
Puddles around my feet, and the voice
Of the first man who cheated on me
And was dumb enough to get caught
Trying to convince me to remain his
Friend.

You can hear young male voices
Shouting profanities because their
Mamas never taught them no better
As they surround me and make
Me their victim.

Making me a victim yet again, and I
Scramble to heal, trying hard to

Survive this and not be another
Statistic having made one dumb
Decision that almost cost me my
Life.

You can hear Mama's voice again
Spouting off some bullshit she
Learned from watching Oprah, and
You can hear the faint cry
From my wounded heart
Just begging for a hug as I try to
Convince myself that I didn't
Deserve this.

You can hear Tío's accordion playing
Over the crackling fire as we sing
Drunken Rancheras into the full moon;
And my boyish giggle as he moves his
Hands up under my shirt in the way I'm
Sure he wished my Tía would let him.

You can hear my silent prayers
Of shame asking for forgiveness
On the night I learned how to
Masturbate to the thoughts of Tío's
Mustache on my chest when he
Would kiss my nipples.

You can hear Selena's voice and
Botines stomping a cumbia on the
Dance floor of the Silver Dollar
Filled with men that turn me on
For looking just like Tío — all dirty
In their own special way.

You can hear cum splattering
Onto the walls of my stomach
As I swallowed the "love" of the

First straight man I ever scored
And the sounds of wasted, sacred
Life coating my rectum because
If he wanted to use a condom, he'd
Sleep with his girlfriend.

I do not bleed for being full of
Life, I simply spill forth the blood
Of my ghosts that lurk inside of
Me just begging to be heard from
The pit of my stomach through my
Hollow frame.

And their sounds echo so loudly
That sometimes I can't think
Straight and I reach through them
And try to pull out art, but even
That doesn't work sometimes.

And their sounds echo so loudly
That sometimes I can't think
Straight and I reach through them
And try to pull out art, but even
That doesn't work sometimes.

On quiet, lonely nights like this
You hear the noises, all milling
Around and bouncing off of my
Heart. You hear them banging
Against my lungs leaving them
Sore like a cigarette hangover.

The sounds are sometimes so
Crippling that they bring me to
My knees in prayer, hoping to
God that I'm not crazy, and that
They will eventually fade away
With time making room for real
Life to grow.

MEMORY

Me acuerdo
a mother's stomach
loose & stretch marked
like a wet toalla rolled
into fist & abandoned
in a dingy corner
y el sonido de perro
growling from your gut
the only hint of sacrifice
done too often & discreetly
as long as children were fed

You took headaches
instead of lovers to bed
ignored your body
& its hungers

Sí, me acuerdo, amá
con mucha pena
those anemic holidays
all of us pretending
que todo estaba bien
celebrating at the house
of a church going friend
porque no teníamos dinero

Still a plastic K-mart X-mas tree
made its yearly debut
in her mismatched trinkets
a Rudolph without his red-nose
paper ornaments made in school
& a broken Jesus in his manger
looking rather forlorn y perdido
under such bleak circumstances

me acuredo, aunque no quiero
the college visits desde Dallas

cloaked in my daughter shame
when I saw you too grateful
head bent like a wilted tulip
eating fried tamales from a plato
not your own
& they smiled eagerly

Rosary clinging monjas & sweaty
palmed padrecitos con sus biblias
only too pleased with themselves
as they hand you, again, two H-E-B
brown paper bags of donated groceries
in exchange for your eternal humility

It continues... a stripping & whipping
of a people who carry his cross of misery

I knew this, long before I gave him up
I called him just another skinny flaco
with hippy hair & a heroin addict's cuerpo
& this earned me a severe threat of chingazo
from you, my mother who protected this ideal son
yet, his whose own heavenly father, I remind you,
left him abandoned, like us, in this mundo

Me acuerdo, amá, de veras, me acuerdo
walking downtown, having left behind
the hospital tiled floors of a project home
where under our tore-up Payless shoes
we heard the crunch & squish of cucaracha
& dad wanting to crush you en la misma manera

But we ran & for a whole night we walked lost
trying to stay awake as we yawned in the stench
of sleepy winitos & high-heeled prostitutas
cuz we ran & we ran when fists hammered
& his words ricocheted against our water-
stained walls

& everything stunk worse than blankets
of piss & tears & the blood he drew
from your woman's face & that mouth of yours
& you wondered how I came to be
an hocicona

I make communion
or is it community?
in this shared past
so I too go hungry
much like you did
only this fast
is my prayer
without regret
& I am filled

OBESAS VUELTAS DE LA VIDA

quisiera penicilina a esta hora
un trago de tequila para mis venas rotas
un antídoto al recuerdo de tus cejas
veneno contra el sudor de tus palmas

palabras para asesinar a la musa
hoguera para incinerar noches difuntas
un texto bíblico para justificar defectos personales
jugo contra la caspa del cabello
del aborto a tu recuerdo
agua bendita contra la sed por un consuelo

las vueltas de la vida son tan obesas
apenas parpadeo y la tristeza
se estaciona desahuciada sobre mi pecho
volviéndose mi dueña

las veces que nuestra historia he expulsado
las horas añorando los años condenado
pagar de nuevo el precio al contado
como cuando te tenía

atropellado por las vueltas de la vida
entre hombres, poemas y sida
traigo empolvadas las manos de reproches

sólo eso me queda
reclamarte por dejarme ir
quedarte allí sentado mientras yo me revelaba
a mensajes opresivos llamándote mi condena

después de una larga espera
renunciaste a tu amor por mí
uniéndote a una ella
lavándote lo que dejé en ti

LORENZO HERRERA Y LOZANO

BROKEN SWEAT AND DREAMS

FUCK'D XICANA

Damn, this finger of time
strumming us along
for six years on
steel guitar strings
playing the song of us

shamelessly, wasting our Sundays
on Hollywood video marathons
munching on palomitas
drenched in Tapatío sauce
days when *shelter* meant
a kiss on the neck
protection your hand
cupping my stomach

such little physical difference
between our first beso & the last
'cept the lack of your 22 yr. old baby fat
that once plumped your bronze cheeks
& for me,
the one cana
or two or three
that maliciously greeted me
with white grins upon turning 30

But we were different by the end.

Still—tell me—there was la música
between us, sometimes out of tune,
but always floating in the background…

Not the Mexican *ay qué sad* songs
the ones you belted when you couldn't talk
when you just didn't have las ganas
cuando Chente, Lola & Paquita
said it all for you
tan dramatically
no, no, I'm talkin' about
the other kind of harmony…

Pero, así nomás...
we parted, mamas,
miscarriage of a future
full of that sickness,
pregnant with our mentiras,
& this love you chose to abort
cuando esa noche
you didn't come home
when you didn't
remember...
Home
cuz she offered you porn
& an easy going time
anything to get you on all fours
Easy
Easy
Xicana fuckin'
Easy
Easy
cuz you were "living another reality"
I see you still all cracked & torn
& your lackluster silver belly ring
& your mouth on her... & then me?

& me too
& me too
all fucked up & raw
& nah...
ain't got no excuse
only shame
for going primal
fightin' dirtier
hatin' on you & her
& me too
& me too
Where's my feminist movement now?
When I call your new lover "bitch"
Where's my race progressiveness?

When I call her "black bitch"
Where's my body image consciousness?
When I call her "fat black bitch"
Where's my love of all our queer sisters?
When I... "#@^&%!*&^$@*!@*&^!*^%%^!"

So it's just like that...
Fuck the hard earned politics,
Fuck friends, fuck family,
cuz everyday I'm feeling sick
Fuck a higher education,
Fuck the so-called community,
Fuck you, &, damn... fuck me.
Fucking me
Fucked me
& this fucked up Xicana bullshit
we did to one another
is worse than a bad-trip
on your mj brownies

& I almost did succeed
before I even learnt the name
of that Mayan diosa—Ixtab
I begged for her then
placed my bloodied mouth at her feet
freeway speeding
sleeping pill popping
planning to offer sacrifice
if she'd just get the traffic
moving along the pinche I-10
cuz if I make it past Arizona
I swear, I'm gonna, I'm gonna...

But Ixtab hears another prayer
cuz I know your guilty atheist heart
prayed hard,
& they prayed,
& I prayed...
for my dead momma

You brought me back with another lie
"Baby, we'll make everything all right…"
I know I need to believe this
believe anything porque este dolor
says it's done been over

So la diosa releases the rope
rejects my light-skinned neck
refuses to take this broke
daughter
home

& mi amor
not a problem
I made home with you
or that
I made you my home
it's that you made me home-
less than nothing
after everything

Por favor, no protest rally
outside my door please
I know when I've been a fucked-up Xicana
but I'm checking myself
so I don't check out permanently
gnawing on this bone of memory
chupando, chupando, chupando,
chupando, chupando, chupando
on what was six years ago…
all six strings snapped…

…don't hear our music no more

ADELINA ANTHONY

NEWFOUND RELIGION

if I had you
I would write on you
I would climb you
touch you
feel you

sodomize my lips
with your fingers
if you were mine

if I belonged to you
I would praise god for you
I would lather up your faith
with all my fears
keep you here

I would raise hell for you
leave other men for you
delete them from my cell
de-friend them on MySpace
dance on their graves dressed in red
only for you

bury every saint I own for my carnal sin
sneeze out loud
eat with my mouth open
shave my chest
whip my back
lick the cross
confess my love for yours

I would lose weight for you
shave my head for you
let you photograph me naked
in church parking lots
let the preachers gawk

I would worship you
vindicate you
rebuild you a hymen from
broken sweat and dreams
make you a virgin for me

WITHDRAWAL

I watched the sun rise on your stubble
I watched the sky go from twinkling
Texas twilight to gorgeous Autumn
Morning in the last hour I knew I had
To spend in your arms, before
The alarm clock sounded and you
Would be taken from my bed.

I let you hold me through the night
And committed your sleep sounds
To memory as you slowly drifted
Into slumber at my side— your hip
Fitting perfectly like a puzzle piece
Against mine.

You woke me up with a gentle
Kiss, not even having the
Patience to wait until I woke up
And brushed the sleep out of
My mouth. You kept kissing
Until you climbed on top of me
And put your nose to my chest
To breathe me in.

You said that my clothes smelled
Of the fabric softener that filled
The air in your grandma's house.
You took comfort in that and I
Caught you smelling me over and
Over when I wasn't looking.

I let you examine my body with
Your strong hands as I rested
My head in the pillow and you
Firmly massaged my back,
Running your fingers down my
Spine and caressing my "sensual
Spots" with extra care.

In one night you managed to
Replace a world of mixed signals
And unspoken feelings with pure
Desire taking in every bit of me
Because you knew it was what you
Wanted and your lips and teeth
And hands and legs clearly
Communicated that all night.

I like this distraction. I crave you.
I curse the alarm clock that
Rings too loud and takes you from
Me. I want to spend more time
Getting lost in your eyes. I want
To stay under the covers until the
Day turns to night and into day again.

RELEASING THE X

Herrera y Lozano:	today I give you back your name no longer are you the pinche el arrastrado canalla aborrecido fucker
Anthony:	today I give you back your name no longer are you the hija de su chingada puta pendeja mentirosa desgraciada
Foxx:	today I give you back your name no longer are you the punk asshole closeted mother fucker
Herrera y Lozano:	no today I'll call you Juan
Anthony:	Carolina
Foxx:	Mocha

TRAGIC BITCHES PLAYLIST

The following songs were incorporated into the performance of
Tragic Bitches:

Song Title	Artist	Album
Alma Adentro	Lourdes Pérez	*Selections from Tres Oraciones*
Buttons	Pussycat Dolls	*PCD*
Crazy (Live)	Norah Jones	*Deep Cuts: Norah Jones*
Duke of Earl	Gene Chandler	*The Duke of Earl*
Échame a Mí la Culpa	Tania Libertad	*Desde el Auditorio Nacional*
Erotic (Sex Book Mix)	Madonna	*Sex Book*
Girls Just Want to Have Fun	Cyndi Lauper	*She's So Unusual*
La Isla Bonita	Madonna	*True Blue*
Lip Gloss	Lil Mama	*Voice of the Young People*
Los Laureles	Linda Ronstadt	*Canciones de Mi Padre*
Maldición Ranchera	Amalia Mendoza	*El Adiós a Una Reina*
Me and Mr. Jones	Amy Winehouse	*Back to Black*
Mi Cucu	La Sonora Dinamita	*Dinamitazos Tropicales*
Not Ready to Make Nice	Dixie Chicks	*Taking the Long Way*
Olvidarte	Ricardo Arjona	*Solo*
Para Saciar Mi Sed	Tania Libertad	*Mexican Divas, Vol. 2*
Pelea de Gallos	María de Lourdes	*La Canción Mexicana*
Por Mujeres Como Tú	Pepe Aguilar	*Por Mujeres Como Tú*
Qué Hiciste	Jennifer López	*Como Ama Una Mujer*
Say It Right	Nelly Furtado	*Loose*
Si Tú No Estás	Rosana	*Lunas Rotas*
Si Tú No Vuelves	Miguel Bosé f. Shakira	*Papito*
Soledad	Chavela Vargas	*Chavela at Carnegie Hall*
Tarde	Ricardo Arjona	*Sin Daños a Terceros*
Te Sigo Amando (Inst.)	Juan Gabriel	*Te Sigo Amando*
Throb	Janet Jackson	*Janet*

Tus Desprecios	Selena	*Amor Prohibido*
While My Guitar Gently Weeps	Martin Luther McCoy McCoy	*Across the Universe Soundtrack*
Yo No Fui	Pedro Infante	*50 Años, Las Consagradas*

ADELINA ANTHONY

Adelina Anthony is a self-identified Xicana-Indígena lesbian multi-disciplinary artista. The themes in her works address colonization, feminism, trauma, memory, gender, race/ethnicity, sexuality, in/migration, health, land/environment, and issues generally affecting the lesbian/gay/bisexual/transgender/two-spirited communities. She believes access to a progressive education, transgressive art, therapy and other healing methods empowers both individuals and communities to make healthy and transformative life choices. (The key, claro, is sticking to those choices... maybe it's one of the reasons we need the rituals of arte in our lives?)

As for her art making, she deftly utilizes critical comedy or dramatic force to impact her many audiences. Adelina has over 17 years of stage experience and has garnered Best-Actress nominations in comedy and drama. This prolific artist has been recognized by her communities and critics as one of the leading solo performers of her generation. Adelina has been featured in *Colorlines Magazine, Frontiers IN L.A. Magazine, Adelante Magazine, Lesbian News, Texas Monthly Magazine, Bitch Magazine, Queer Codex: ROOTED!* (*allgo*/Evelyn Street Press) and other publications. For more visit adelinaanthony.com

DINO FOXX

Dino Foxx, born and raised in San Antonio, is a nationally presented actor, singer, dancer, writer, spoken word poet, hip-hop artist, arts educator and activist. He is a founding member of the Tragic Bitches Poetry Collaborative, a company member with Jump-Start Performance Co. and an emcee with the band The Push Pens. His poetry, which follows "themes of family unity and disunity, ethnic bonds and divisions, assimilation and displacement as well as sexuality and love" (Andrés Duque of Blabbeando), has been published in such collections as *Mariposas: A Modern Anthology of Queer Latino Poetry* (Floricanto Press 2008), the 19th issue of *Suspect Thoughts: A journal of subversive writing* (2007) and the radical Queer People of Color Anthology, *Queer Codex: Chile Love* (*allgo*/Evelyn Street Press). Foxx is also in the process of publishing his first collection of poetry through Korima Press. In his spare time, Dino enjoys fire-eating, knitting, hoop-dancing and is now exploring the world of bear-lesque as a member of Stars and Garters Burlesque.

LORENZO HERRERA Y LOZANO

Lorenzo Herrera y Lozano is a queer Xicano writer of Rarámuri descent born in San José, CA and raised in Estación Adela, Chihuahua. A St. Edward's University Masters of Liberal Arts graduate, he is the author of the Lambda Literary Award-nominated *Santo de la Pata Alzada: Poems from the Queer/Xicano/Positive Pen* (Evelyn Street Press), editor of *Queer Codex: Chile Love* (*allgo*/Evelyn Street Press) and *Queer Codex: ROOTED!* (*allgo*/Evelyn Street Press), as well as the forthcoming *Joto: An Anthology of Queer Ch/Xicano Poetry* (Kórima Press). A member of the Macondo Writing Workshop, his work also appears in *Mariposas: A Modern Anthology of Queer Latino Poetry* (Floricanto Press), *ZYZZYVA: the journal of West Coast writers and artists*, and *Yellow Medicine Review: A Journal of Indigenous Literature, Art, and Thought*. For more visit: herreraylozano.com